A BRAND NEW BEGGAR

A BRAND NEW BEGGAR

A. L. Nielsen

STEERAGE PRESS

~ Steerage Press ~
steeragepress.com
Boulder, Colorado and Normal, Illinois

Welcome to the lifeboat party.

August Darnell

ACKNOWLEDGMENTS

Some of these poems appeared in earlier versions in *Exchange Values, i.e. Reader, The GW Review, Wooden Teeth, Poet Lore, Yellow Field, House Organ* and *Generator*. The author thanks the editors of these publications for their support.

Other poems first appeared in the Italian journal of American Studies *RSA*, translated by Marina Morbiducci.

Thanks to Ariel Braverman for her beautiful cover design. And thanks to Anna Everett for lending a hand.

CONTENTS

A BRAND NEW BEGGAR

I

Cecil's Train Set

for C. S. Giscombe

In at last night from
Chicago
Lining red-eyed track
Smothered clack
Of post prairie ties

Ribonned cross
Sleepless eyes
Out the window what hard
Highways

To bypass

Elevators gone from grain
Exploded village backside
Broken by abandoned
Overpass

Uneven trees gone to rail beds
Even sleepers belittled by overriding

There is no reparative
Roundhouse
Rather infinite
Rehearsal

It was towns
Brought the time
Across the prairies

Bridge passage
To switch
That trains us

To read that lost
Phrase

Balanced on your bicycle
Carry it to Canada

Commuter Flight

To find still
              Vast tracts
       Of nothing from the air

Bursts of land so flat
              You want to put anything other
       Than yourself down there

A lone rancher halts his pick-up
              Stares skyward praying
       We might set a mall on his land

A mind strays

To think her on the fly
              At this altitude as a way of saving
       This plane against the day's rising spumes

Flying between the Rockies and a soft voice
              An image I would like
       To light upon

An idea of an actual woman
              Glad to find at thirteen thousand feet
       An effect in the real world of my body

An idea of her on a lake in the South
              Ripples the surface she stares across
       To follow the shadow of a winging thing overhead

What word of her comes to mind here
What every rider below already knows
As I bank left and look to the mountains

"You must throw your heart over

The obstacle before you jump."

Our shadow races the foothills
            Crosses a stock tank ringed with thirst
        And so approaches what she must feel

I think her at this angle
            And then
        Think the man who thinks this thing

Leap in the plane trying
            To right the attitude
        Of approach
Out of our various countryside

Could anyone in Tennessee
            Imagine Wyoming as seen
        From such a height

Could anyone imagining Tennessee
            Set down in this place
        Without jarring himself

Plane wheels
            My skies fill with snow
        Capped tan breasts

I reach a hand out the window to the thin cold
Come back with a word the French use for "home"

This little will do me
Till she can

Anna

A is for an

Other

Part of our

Name a

Part or

Conjoined we

Remain

An

Article

Aldon D.

My father's lung

Concussed

Nebraska air

Rushed to the front

Punched out of Belgian mud

Was it the same

Shelling shook

Oppen

Shook me

Loose

It was not this sky

Wounded them

Both

Not this sky

"Spread so thin

That the situation

Was eerily

Precarious."

To owe nothing

Whatsoever

To the fact

Of this shell

Save life

And all

Its fortunate

Accidents

Was the fate

Faced so many

Sons

It wasn't they

Stayed alive

For us

But they

Stayed

Anna

I would have liked to have
            Written you
Sooner than this
Or later than that

As now I would
Like to write you
            For sheerest love of your line

I would like to have written you
Before you read this

            To have tried with my tongue
            And unsure hand
            In how many languages
            You might be
            Accomplished

To have pried with my tongue
Among your many meanings

I would have liked to find
Among your many leanings
This inclination

            To lay
            Myself down

Or better to have been

        Here all along

Sunken Gardens

That tree from which my mother
Had had
To talk me down
Looked down
Into the sunken bowl
Of the garden
It was called
Which when
Filled with snow I'd
Walked
Confidently into

What hellfires burned
After came of that Baptist
Earth fed
The tree that grew
Downward through
Snow rooting soul
Between sky and sunken
Gardens

41

Sweet crude

Target air

Significant strike

                              We went in with a bunch of guys
                              Like Christmas lights

Acquired aircraft
At some point you become comfortable
At some pont you become an unfriendly
Huge fireball

                    Technology transfer

We ran a touchdown
And the enemy didn't show up

We're on that problem big time

We want to talk to that battery
At an interval we can predict

                              Continuous
                              Breaking developments

Intermittent
Leaders
Spoke holy places

The market continues its wild ride

Continuous coverage of carpet bombing will resume after this

            We get more punch per bomb

A struggle to the last child

                        Sell on the rumor
                        Buy on the news

IN A MACRO SENSE
                        I'm getting some information in my
                        other ear

SO FAR IT'S A BLOWOUT

Seven Series

1

An end to all this

        Eschatology

2

In tag football each player wears a white
Towel tailing
In tag-team wrestling next to nothing
Is worn
In Wernicke's area we play
Tails out
Untaped   untagged

3

When I fell on a rusty nail I was rushed
To the doctor's office for a shot
To prevent lockjaw
It left me prosaic

4

You close your eyes
While we kiss I move
All the furniture
Later falling
Onto the couch
You tell me you want
Another one of those good kisses
You know
I've got

5

I have
To hurry

Here

They close
The dictionaries
At seven

6

Exploring the tailings
Vast heaps of them above the town
Water seeping through poisonous
Radiant
They subside into forms too late
To pack them back into the hole
Without what was extracted

Rules parked rusting at the edge
Children of a kiss climbing on the mounds
Glowing
In mutant morning
Their little black boxes emitting acquisitive blips
Their faces register

7

Moving, Yours

After your chest
Finding your rain where it ran
From breast to belly
Was like finding the cat
Licking long after at your thumb
Print in the mirror
Or one of your nails
Sheltering itself in the sheets
Waiting
To scratch your name
From my neck
Or your music
Webbing the corners
Where I'd never dusted

Catching up
I've carried it out
Set it beside your annuals
Which this year sprang out
Of the yard next door
To be carried off with the rest
Of what we've left

But it works its way back
Taking up

It rings the windows at night
When I am beside myself
With sleep
Wreathing the spots where you'd
Nippled the night against starlight
It tides me over

Till the day strokes
Back upchannel

From the Eastern Shore lighting upon your last
Hairs hung from my blind side
Like a hungering comer
Fastening on a limb
As easement

Waking
I am up against it
Even though what it attaches to
Has taken itself off
It tends to me still
It is a poem that conceals its leanings
As it reveals itself
There against the darkness
Of a turned shoulder

It is a pumping clock that concedes
To its own works
A certain sluggish accuracy
While it goes through its motions
Beating down
To unfurnished ground

Getting up

Leaving
I turn
Cornering against the light
Our bed tips dangerously from the roof where I've roped it
Secrets glare out from the tied down trunk
Tired and wary they hunker down in boxes
Packed against the spare

Your plants lean across the seat
Rustling at my ear
Their leaves and tendrils

Traffic in tedious signs
Breaking through the static
I can just make it out

II

from KANSAS

"Nor with the power of American vocables
would I arm you in Kansas"

Charles Olson

Kaman's hawk riffing

      With the wind

The roar in wings

      When Jay's hawk answers

*

[Frank]

The
Mothers

Of necessity

Sang

Kansas
Kansas
do-do-dun to-to

It was
For them
An invention

*

They warned of burning

      Kansas

Roiling plates

      Planes of

Climate change

Antebellum broiling

*

What's wrong with Kansas

That thousands

Crossed to vote

To burn against freedom

The very idea

*

Stirring Brownian

Counter motions

Continental drift split

A nation along

Fault lines of fury

*

Sheet lightning announces

An engine

Across those same lanes

Outracing its whistle

*

There's no

Their there

*

I'm new here

Gil Scott-Heron

Whispers from a passing window

In Brown's Lawrence

*

Brakhage born boy

Soprano orphan

Sang frames

Painted his cell

III

At Desk

The numbered bricks out of sequence
Arch across my window somehow
Still hold to the key hold
Over glassine space
Whether because the child who chalked them
Or the mason paid scant
Attention
The work at hand holds up
The space opens between us
As if by glass the faulty numeration
Corrects itself as if by air
The brick does not crush the glance
That passes beneath to see on that
Measure of glass through all that passes
Driven beams that corner night
Cross eyes with me
The hail that falls toward
A new neighbor moving by stages
Upstairs a stereo shakes the whole
But it still holds together on the vibrant pane
Without leaves no
Leaves as if
Some as if from out Nebraska
Where hail insurance is impossible to get
And cows are killed and corn
Fields stripped clean and Bruce
My best friend from Kindergarten who couldn't
Turn a cart-wheel but could
Find one stone big as a baseball
And got to show it off on the radio
Kept me from renting such a place
With leaves to brush against all this
Is in my eyes in the window reverberating against
The trash-bin out front and the children
Who can count out of order as well as I

On these bricks turning cart-wheels
Beneath the lightning flash signing
In shades intermittently why
Don't you take the whole thing
Apart and put it back together right
Mister and they count as well as they appear
In me and in no other order
Than that of their arrival
Striving to be taken down
Along with window and all it can
Contain can be mortared in and set
Safe from storm at desk
A car left at the curb stripped
Trickling across the pane smears the page
Outside and inside sucking at the same scene
Hail hitting one side music trembling from
The other so much I must keep up with
So much to keep up
The numbers running back and forth offer themselves
As guides measures to be resisted leaning
The tendency to fall cementing
Them the desire to come apart holding
Me here behind the numbers so much to take
Down before light comes unswitched
Separating everything
To its side

Hidden Lake

Explaining away a lake
They lose   they balance
They lose   they name
          Lodge
Cleft in   the mountain
Echoes take a breather
Advertise springs
Water gets second wind
Hunches sheltering
In the cleft
Bears against spinning block
A bowl is turned out
Tries to look like surrounding
Whistles itself like a lake
On a mountaintop that doesn't know
It's   hidden
They lose   theyselves

A place could drive around for years
Wondering   what's up
Eyeing huge trees fallen across the path
As something to be sawn someday
A good project for the kids to climb
So high they cannot see the way they have come
A memory they can turn
While foot falters mid-air
Drowning at altitudes to hear
A boy scout say peeing into the lake
Thirteen thousand feet above
Sea level "this sucks" and
Not be concerned about his language
Echoing
Still
Whistling the shape of a troop
A shape of no animal that comes here

To peer at itself frozen in the surface
Of that piddling lake
The shapes that take longer at altitudes where
To rise requires special instruction
From ice to stream an endless wait
Where snow takes all day
And cakes
Fall precipitously
And that lake
That does not feed at this level
Road turning
From declivities
Signs posted against trespass
Chasm fuming above
The treeline foments
Lichen fumbles
Lakeward divides
Drifting continent
At this level
Colorado Springs

Geotropism

A flower
Bubbles on the lips

Opens with night
Turning toward black
Sky

Holding out petals
For what might be caught
From air

Roots thrust back
Through the throat like needles

Coming to bone
They scrape their way
Through fine powder

In time tip
Into heart

And opening there
Drink in the dark

Above the flower
Whispers

Trust

Trust

Rivers

Between rock and a heard place
A point amplified

In improvisation
Reedy scales

Readiness in waiting
Weighing the moment

An idea
Pitched in the rest

Taken up by
The rest

Rests

The finite work of morning
Refrains

Evening
The score

Small Song

Really doesn't matter
  Which way I call
Night still
  Has a long way to fall

Really doesn't matter
  How long I pray
Night still
  Will soon give to day

Really doesn't matter
  How hard I sing
Night still
  Removes every thing

Really doesn't matter
  What I might will
Night
Still

Smaller Still

When he had heard
Every note

He directed
Himself

To silence

A Farfisa for Margo

The chord that carried us
        Carried too
                This claim
On our hearing

Our own
        Demands
                Of ourselves

Your fingers always
        The compass
                Of our composing

Exercised

Next to the parking lot
At the foot
Of the mountain

Another mountain

This one
With handholds

Personal Note

Beats me
How it happened when you left
There was this bone behind
In the bed

Too short to be mine and outside
Brittle
Against my back   were you walking
When you left   you'd warned for years
You'd one day walk but I don't remember
I was asleep when you left
Are you missing

Something

Combing Paris

Lighted panels acting
Created Modernism

And a new black leather couch
The real problem was getting it to stick

In some same seine
Part of what makes democracy

The last loss of empire
A pledge from co-religionists

From discrepant depths
Rhyme hidden so deep as to be beyond layered lime

Lines of estimation
From an abandoned book of design

An artisanal cover
The gift of a blank book

Designed to sell design
Designated black looks

Something was amiss on this mountain
The building flocks of imperium

Darkened its nether side
Nether ride

Higher Math

Geese flock over
Their familiar equation
A is greater than B

I wait unlicensed
In the caesura of their seasons
Scrawling with my shotgun in mid-mud

Out of season they fly by
Again A is
Less than B

We are evened
North and South
The geese and I

Silence of the Iambs

Every now
        and again
I take my I
        out
For a walk and a rinse

I is a mother
        So say
                My neighbors
In an obligatory
        Obligato
Of call and remorse

I tell them to
        Put it where
                The pod don't play

As the whether
        Or not balloons
                Tear loose
From their subsidies

I hear voices
        From the other's side
As if someone were
        Reading a poem

The Collector of Wrong Figures

I take them down as they are
Reduced and reproduced
Little caring for application
Or significance

But then something
I can't see
Outside asserts itself and figures inflate
My attention

Averted
The great applicator takes them up outside
And all
And then

The blown figure among men
Uncorrected
The effect of the thing within it
Passed around

With refreshments at the meeting
Where it will be decided
How and how much and
From whom

Brought up and examined
Evidence for or
Against the semblance
Of an outside

Works its way into the graph
Unrolled may bubble there
Or evaporate as fingers
Follow greedily over the space

Without
Meaning
I provide
Fat for the plans

A rationale from which
Overruns may proceed
Perforated printout
Along a beach stroll

Husband and wife standing
One to each side oiling up
As explanation is proffered
Just so the kids understand

The board votes to
Execute a program
Punching later
My fingers wear while the bubble

Passes unnoted
Family irretrievably lost
A missing value
Nothing to take its place

But the period finds its way
Into the scheme of things
Adding itself over again to
No effect

The error statement
Validity checks

I dam it up
Take it home
Put it in its place
Next to

CAN YOU DRAW THIS MAN and

I CAN SHOW YOU HOW TO MAKE IT BIG
IN UPHOLSTERY

At a Glance

The stomach sentence
Men of his stature did not lie
Shot to death in puddles at this hour

O boat tea

Mesmerized by discomfort
Memory diminished him

The English pronounced
As well they would

I mean a nation

Bashed
The edge of the fields
Falls
Unlikely Canada refuses forces

"The pearl of Africa"
No listener on the hill

"The bad habit of suffering injustice in silence"

The opportunities error brings

That wonder is in the center
Bodies make things move

Across a road trucks take in
All works of good will border on

But although these are
Stomached
How you construe consequence

Live up to your crimes

Climb clime

An Assumption of Angels

"The said must be torn from the unsaid."

Roland Barthes

Because we have so far been
Unable to hold an explanation to ourselves
There are men mounted in the trees outside
Counting our children
As they pass
Explanations slip down drains and wash
Through streams beneath our streets
Whispering from man-holes
Dead children with unused names
The men tire of counting and dig
Their fingers into the bark
The trees dig into sewers taking up the lost names
Humming them to the men hidden in their limbs

There is nothing that can be said
So terrible that it cannot occur

We sit on our porches hiding behind the news
Wondering what any of us could need so badly
That he would tear it apart in some deaf field
Where it would lie for days till rain washed its parts clean
And weeks later the name would be found again
Lodged against the grates nearly home
Bubbling like ripped and free-floating plastic

In one bright corner of the city
Someone we have eaten with
Caresses an idea he cannot speak to us
He counts our children too
They chant in the courtyard
Jumping the length of the line

They use to link themselves together
Counting off the gone
They promise each other
"If you jump high enough
God will pluck you up and
Make you an angel like the others."

"Why did they all have the same name?"

"All angels have the same name."

How should we explain ourselves to them
But by teasing free this same truth
They leap higher and higher toward

See in this an assumption of angels
Premature
Into heaven
We could not say to them
Our attention wanders as you do
And some more attentive one of us
Takes you to punish us
We could not tell them
There is nothing any of us can think
So dread that we couldn't find another
To join us in the thinking and doing of it

We pluck up the name from the grates
Call it and all the children
Even the airborne
Turn their heads toward us

Is this how it happens

Carole Denise
Angela Denise
Darlenia Denise
Brenda Denise

Walking to the store
Walking home from The Wall
Walking from The Hill Center
From the Safeway
Under the sleeping men in trees

Nothing so unspeakable we won't one day see it
And lay it to a phantom
Nothing we can say so terrible
It cannot occur
No explanations to hold against ourselves

An assumption of angels

IV

from GHANA

Accra in my throat
A philosophy
A flight
A float
Beats back
History
To first's shore
Up
Amazing
Space
Grace
To land
A full-throated cry

*

"Time was
crucified
on the cross"
So Sun Ra says
Hence the "X"
"What time is it?"
We shouted
Then
When
If time is on the cross
What do they serve
In the GOD IS GREAT CHOP BAR

*

Sitting on the coast in Accra
I read
"We are passing the coast of Africa"
But that was written
To Tom Raworth
(Who I saw just last week)
Some forty odd years ago

*

Word arrives that Jesse Helms has died
Tolson's Africa shakes off a fly

*

At Independence Square
The Black Star arches above
America's Independence Day

*

But home is in flames
I hear
Through African rains

*

Lizard doing his morning pushups

*

I take book to beach
For cooling comfort
Cold prose
High tide
Cattle come lowing
Along the sand
Sounding in common

*

Chickens in the trees
A sight I'd never see
As a child
In Nebraska
Perhaps because
No trees

*

Illegible sand writing
Stretches recognition
Till it snaps
In bands of illuminated sea

*

Gratitude for such wary
Signage as
Sings to me
Each morning
Such as this
Muddy Waters pouring
From seaside speakers
Sounding
Homecoming baptism

*

Blocks stacked neatly
In ambition
One day to be
A habitation
No house
The city of lizards
Offers me citizenship

*

Blind shoes hang
By the roadside
The footloose drive by
A man necklaced with
Athletic shoes
Repeating
"Foot
Foot"
Followed a day later by
"Socks
Socks"

*

A race on its
Last lap
Danced dying across
These souls
Centuries past

*

The official language
Was postcolonial
But there was a coup
Now everyone speaks

*

Angel hair glow
Rising from the foam
Nkrumah's furniture
From his dorm room
Lincoln University U.S.A.
Where he sat with C.L.R. James
Carefully preserved in
The museum
As outside
Also carefully preserved
The destroyed likeness
Statue overthrown by
Subsidized mob

*

In a room in
Kokrobitey
Silk screens multiply
Obama
From across the sea
Whose father was from
Across the continent

*

Omar Epps
Introduces himself
To me in the market
Surprised
As I am
To find himself
Talking to Elvis

V

Ghost Dance Slide Show
(Mama, Don't Take My Ektachrome Away)

Untitled Slide

That is a deep blue immensity
Of nothing projecting from its frame
To engulf the screen and half the room
Beyond
I didn't take this
The people at the processing lab added it
They always add one blue immensity
Whether to protect my slide beneath it in the box
Or simply to give me all my film and
Money's worth they've never said
I never ask
They look at me as if to say
We give one of these to everybody
As an ideal
The better to measure your own

School Slide

These unbearable trees green against the film
In this near winter picture
The line of tree thinning to rock and shadow
Sun scaling stone and lichen behind the fur
Of your coat and the stretch of sweater where weave
Nearly parts across resurgent nipple glistens
Tongue touched black beneath white wool
Where I have been only this morning
And there in the corner red in bunches
Splayed along branches are those berries
Are those the berries my mama warned
Years ago were poison

Zoo Slide

Here you are seen with an ear
Before a gardenia looking like Lady Day
Used to look out of cover sketches
At me the same sparkle of lip
Put there by the artists only yours is a matter of sun
Glossing chocolate
Lips parting in mid-surprise as
The hippopotamus yawns behind you

Intermission

Some nights I run through these slides
Try to animate by rushing the least
Flickering show of you and some nights stop
Altogether between frames to find
If any subliminal message has inserted
Itself and it has
And that
Is you too
The closed eyes scanning
In head held pride of having made
Something of cloth or clay
Or of me
The place you want me to feel in
For the meaning of those things
You speak out of sleep
That clinging of inner arm to outer breast
Swell as you rise to say them
That I kiss
Easing you back to whatever dream
Of making the place
That lies by my side when you've left for the day

There is the light that plays in the slides
And before it plays there again
The darkness of intermission
The machine is doing something
With that driven whir

It is repeating secrets you told
When we were asleep
I go to the next room
Whisper in the same place

Zoo Slide Two

"It's light there!"
"It's light there!"

You and your sister
Mouth in the screen
Fingers pointing out ahead
To me

I was angling for the sun at my back
I had tried to get you under that tree
As before
But your sister said the shade was all wrong
The two of you would be lost

Someone took your sister to the zoo

Every time she visited
I'd left my light
Meter behind
From now on it would be me

But what was that direction the two of you
Preferred
Fingering a beam coincident
With the breadth of the barrel
Toward that blaze of filament

Neon-blue toucan

Puzzled suddenly
I pull the slide and you are gone
Both back to the bulb

Bare tongues outside

The aviary

These cordless electric angels
Can go anywhere

Sculpture Garden Slide

They can't be seen but all around you
To my rear the statues stand you
Are seated in a wooden slat-backed chair your back
To my camera facing into a corner where
Walls meet I was careful to exclude both
Sky and ground
I wanted neither to interfere with the walls
You and I faced
Nor to include any suggestion of statuary
I waited till even their shadows withdrew
From the frame so that they would not seem
To comment on my composition
And your back was meant to appear
As placed by some inconsequential teacher
But your head blurs upward
Listens
To statues clacking all around

Nude Slide

We had been throwing pots and now naked
Threw hand-sized globes of clay at each other
Wet brown balls that on impact took
The shape of whatever was
Aimed at
There's one on the floor with the imprint of an ear
Another stuck to the wall above and behind
Shows signs of both nose and knee
We were alone in the studio with wheels off
Kiln heat reaching for our bodies when
Throwing ourselves on one another
Laughing this was taken by remote control
With a ten second delay on high speed
Ektachrome at f/4 1/60th of a second
By existing light

Was ever a slide so full of itself

Surprised Slide

Myself asleep enlarged
Twenty times
You stole
To the table in darkness
Took and adjusted the camera
Entirely by feel
Finding somehow the right distance
Clicked shutter and strobe
Towards the bed
You caught me cold
Pillowed like some maniac
Coming to a rude conclusion

Pot Slide

I think this is my favorite though you are nowhere
In it but the blanket
You used to wrap your sun drenched self in before passing
The window our neighbors
Could see into on your way to
The kitchen for tea
Me watching all the while the rise and fall
Of thigh transformed to
Waving blue wool
Is stretched from floor and attached to wall
As bottom and background for this slide
Of what I think your best
Pot
The one you drew
Up from a tear drop to a finger
Width neck
I used reflected light to soften the weave
So the glare of glaze would be more
Its own doing
I circled for five shots recording
Each inch in order the colors
You had brought to surface
And fired for more permanence than film
From the five this is the one
That best suggests what cannot be seen
As if your design at this point set
A course that must be followed through
I often wondered if in the hollow interior
Of your work the negative of your figure
Was repeated like threads on the reverse
Of embroidered silk
You wouldn't tell

And I couldn't with whatever light
Eye pressed to that finger mouth
See
It may be that mystery
Holds me on this
My favorite
Even though you are not
In it at all

"Ain't Nothing Like The Real Thing"
(A Slide With Songs)

Alone now with my slide show
I tell myself this is the next best
Thing to being
There with you
So much better than the flat
Photo pressed like someone's prom flowers
Between album leaves
With a sheet stretched for screen
I see your picture hanging on the wall
And multiplied on dust as well in air
I did not see till light
Threw you through it
Sweet air I might step into
Inhale the image or warp it
Across my chest walking through
Hanging gardens toward your inexact
Likeness moving near
Or far for focus
Fit myself into your
Close size and shape
Feel the warm black light of you
Falling on my face
Mouth open to your teeth sing
Baby be home soon

. . . and I followed her to the station

This suitcase intends

      A world

Broke at the clasp

         Grasp

World gone wrong

These rails portend

      A done wrong life

These unintended

      Blues stones

In my passway

      Cinders rasp

         In my draw

Rail against the night

Smokestack steel strings

    Open tuning

        Bottle up and go

She gone

What I loved well

    Booked

In the wake

    Her train

Black rain

    Conveyance

        To freezing ties

Blinding

Binding

Dry ice

A. L. NIELSEN

A. L. Nielsen is the author of the previous collections of poetry *Heat Strings, Evacuation Routes, Stepping Razor, VEXT, Mixage* and *Mantic Semantic*. His work has been included in *Best American Poetry* and has won *Gertrude Stein* awards. His works of criticism include *Reading Race, Writing between the Lines, C.L.R. James: A Critical Introduction, Black Chant* and *Integral Music: Languages of African American Innovation*. His critical work has received the SAMLA Studies Prize, the Kayden Prize, a Gustavus Myers citation, and the Josephine Miles Award. With Lauri Ramey he has edited two anthologies of innovative poetry by African American artists, *Every Goodbye Ain't Gone* and *What I Say*. He is also the editor of *Reading Race in American Poetry* and of Lorenzo Thomas's posthumous work, *Don't Deny My Name*, which won an American Book Award. He is currently the George and Barbara Kelly Professor of American Literature at the Pennsylvania State University, and has also taught at Howard University, UCLA, San Jose State University, and Loyola Marymount University.

Steerage Press

~ *where good books are given berth* ~

_____

Joe Amato, *Big Man with a Shovel*
Chris Pusateri, *Common Time*
Michael Joyce, *Disappearance*
A. L. Nielsen, *A Brand New Beggar*

www.ingramcontent.com/pod-product-compliance
Lightning Source LLC
Chambersburg PA
CBHW031558040426

42452CB00006B/336